Through

Also by David Herd from Carcanet
Mandelson! Mandelson! A Memoir (2005)
All Just (2012)

Through

David Herd
Carcanet
2016

First published in Great Britain in 2016 by
Carcanet Press Limited
Alliance House, 30 Cross Street
Manchester, M2 7AQ
www.carcanet.co.uk

A CIP catalogue record for this book is available from
the British Library: ISBN 9781784102562

The publisher acknowledges financial
assistance from Arts Council England

CONTENTS

WHO LEAVES THE LANGUAGE

WHO LEAVES THE LANGUAGE

It is possible to be precise.

The line is drawn at the AIC, Rosebery Avenue, EC1R.

The building is Taylor House, although it doesn't look much like a house. It has the name House because it *houses* the AIC, as in the verb rather than the noun. It looks through tinted plate-glass windows. To my knowledge there is no sign saying who Taylor was. There are more obvious landmarks. One might notice Finsbury Town Hall, or the various outlets that populate Exmouth Market. We are not far from the City or the British Library. It is at the AIC, however, that the line is drawn, that hour by hour the decision is taken: who leaves the language.

I nearly said judgment.

Enters also.

The AIC is a busy place. There are all the usual security checks so that at the turnstile you offload your belongings, everything you keep in your pockets along with your coat and your bag, like at an airport, and then you go through the metal detector in case you are carrying a knife. But these checks are just routine. Theoretically the AIC is open to the public.

Who constitutes the public is interesting. Actually it is the building's question. Though if public means those who don't have a function in the proceedings then mostly the public isn't there. Really, it is the building's question: who leaves the language. Once through the turnstile you take the lift to a waiting area on the second floor.

This is where the action is, though for the most part the action is waiting. Waiting, it turns out, is what engaging the AIC is principally about. Not waiting as in waiting to go in. More like waiting as an administrative weapon. As if in the absence of any other tactic what somebody once dreamed was an indefinitely enduring holding pen.

Imagine having that dream.

You'd have to have a mind of winter.

For tactic you might think solution. Either way the holding pen is real. It's just that in its thoroughness it functions like a metaphor. Anyway people live there, sometimes for years. There, in abeyance, where the administration dreamed them.

The person principally waiting at the AIC is the appellant. He or she is rarely white. The people waiting with the appellant will be their friends and supporters and when they have some their family. In most cases they will be accompanied by a legal representative, though increasingly this doesn't apply. If they are there, that is – which is to say, if the appellant is in the building. Elsewhere in the AIC is the HOPO, the Home Office Presenting Officer so called, and, though it isn't possible to see them yet, the Judge who is a civil servant also, and who sometimes hears presentations on his own, or her own, and sometimes in the company of a layperson. It is the Judge, sometimes in the company of a layperson, who constitutes the tribunal.

What the tribunal judges is the language. What the tribunal judges with is the language. What the Judge determines when he reaches his determination is by whom the language can be used. What he circumscribes is the polis and what the tribunal constitutes is the primal scene, the setting where the language is formed by expulsion.

I can't say this fully enough.

Witness the AIC.

The AIC's function is as a portal to a 'hostile environment'. I offer it up in quotes because it is enshrined in law, because we have been rendered hostile, and where the hostility settles and finds its focus is as it handles the appellant.

The tribunal is not a court of a record. Nobody here is writing everything down. It is the Home Office Presenting Officer who principally draws the line. That is his job, or her job, their function being to so diminish the appellant that the Judge and his companion can comfortably expel them. Where exactly, nobody knows. This is not the building's question. The building's question is how best to sever any residual linguistic ties, any intimacies that might have formed, so that the tribunal might perform its task, leaving the language unaffected by the process of expulsion.

People spirited away. Barely rendered present in the first place. In the event that an appellant receives relief they are paid in vouchers not cash. So that the currency is like the language, so that the function might be performed, so that as it is determined who leaves the language the language determining goes untouched.

This is the tribunal's job. It is the focal point of all the language, the setting where official hostility achieves full expression in all its multiple forms, where the Presenting Officer asks a series of questions that beggar belief in their disregard for the appellant's actual circumstance, where mistranslation goes wilfully uncorrected, where fundamental documents are routinely withheld. Where the line is drawn. Where the hostile environment is made administratively manifest. Where the language forms by a series of procedures holding intimacy at bay. Where the procedures go unrecorded. Where all the intimacies are lost. Where that tone we live with that claims to represent us is perfected by compulsive use.

Because it doth remove

Those things which

Elemented

The language formed in the act of separation not acknowledging the absence of those it compels to leave, established by the breach, the act of shipping people out

That ourselves know

Witness the language

Driven through

The AIC.

THROUGH

I.

                                        Let's go then
Because if we don't nobody will –
I had this thought for the morning,
We could   concentrate our energies on the movement through
Weigh down on the action
Work out where the word becomes feeling
Through
Step over into the traffic   through.

Not that it has to be a morning thing,
I work late above the dooryard

                                        The sheer distance
                                                    That
                                        Abstract reckoning
                                        For no other reason
                                                The world.
Which is   chatting with you
Watching movies with you
In which the most innocent gesture
                                        Or the smallest forgetfulness
Waiting a letter with

II.

This I can say:
It showed me finally
That the actions of a person
Clear and pale
Thus effectively lost
Witness
The evidence
Calm, unbroken
Occur here.

I can say this in the morning
Nobody statements foreclose
No tribunal today
Not this sunshine
No letter either,
Just some life story
Folded through
Played out piecemeal as
Biography happens:

Steady
Anonymous
Simultaneous
Activity.

I talk to Simon
Simon sets the birdsong out of Peckham
We listen awhile and
Over the traffic
Somebody cultivates
The Old Kent Road –
Which is the way things go
Things go gracelessly   as we go
Aware –
No one asking today
Nobody auditing –
As persons

Standing   still
Which is I submit
The evidence necessary,
Trousers   nothing special
Watching the way
The wind blows
In your telltale shoes,
The case   against
Harbouring affections
In the face of
Politics:

                                        Six
                               Brushed teeth
                       Noticed the world wake
                               All dewy
                            And confused.

                                       Topsy
                                       Turvy.

As these societies became more complex
The need for writing
For administrative purposes
For recording legends

For myths
All dewy
Woke up startled into consciousness
All the evidence today   assembled   argued
Through

III.

MIDNIGHT
And all the while   some kind of
Collective emergency
Leafing through Mayakovsky
I look at politics in poems
Bargains

                                                    struck at dead of night
I'm thinking
            LET'S GET THE TRANSLATION RIGHT SHALL WE
Habiter
From habitation

                                                    I look at politics
                                                    And stones

And use the word advisedly
I use the word 'advisedly' advisedly
Picture us in some kind of ruin
Waiting for the rhetoric to show
Sea whacked
And no-one home
I shake hands with Lucy Williams
You   standing on the battlements
Contemplating the prospect

                                            possibly so.

IV.

And so the sun kicks on.
I think I'll take that document now please
And then   maybe later
We'll come up with some kind of plan
Since this is serious and you're so well dressed
Shoes shined like your life depended on it
In the rubble
Maintenant en Français
Oui   c'est grave.

You say the word 'grave' advisedly,
There is no word for 'all' in English,
Standing   watching the traffic
Waiting for the agencies to show,
Tout   le monde,
Waiting for the world to show
Outside your doorstep
Like lilac like
Standing still and walking
Waiting while the dogwood
At your garden door.

Which it doesn't   happen
The way the lyric steps up all   uninvited
Like lilac   all
You had to do was listen
Waiting in the doorway while
The world rolled past
Some kind of presidency
One by one

I am no recipient of culture
It's an agency thing
I listen to Jarvis
Jarvis Cocker plays
LeRoi Jones

At the doorway singing
Jarvis plays Gill Scott Heron
Collis starts up
Jarvis plays Olson
I had to learn the simplest things last
Not an ocean stretching out beneath my feet
Just that it's a you and I thing
Crossing somewhere
Making an agreement
Following the language
Through

V.

But if we had to start over
Even only air and such
Slate grey April
Nobody roots attached
If we had to start   lengthen bodies out
Set down a canopy   out of nothing
Table something   out of nowhere
Wouldn't it go like this?

This is my question.
I note down books people talk to me:
                              Edward Casey, *The Fate of Place*
Mystic sheer distance
That beautiful abstract reckoning
Sun drift over Camberwell
I write a poem about space

Waiting in case the world
Let's get the implication right shall we
Standing   sampling Massive Attack
Down by the salle d'attente
And we shall construct at variance
Singing in the present participle
Urban today   everybody
Uninvited

Like some kind of document filled with other people's songs
The only surviving parchment of the twenty-first century
Some kind of air crash
In which the only thing remaining
Was a line out of Gertrude Stein
Quoted by Simon Smith
In a train just departed Dartford
Space   of time   filled   with moving

I write a poem about Margate
Folded out toward an abstract reckoning
Assemble this night
In the present participle
Watching the uninvited
As they start to sing
The Wreck of the Deutschland
Set down a canopy out of nowhere
Footage   you are now   exiting   the future.

VI.

So the names roll out again
Dartford, Chennai
The angel in the doorway clicks his teeth
Because here is how he likes it
Dirty intense
Ibuprofen heavy
Thick with song.

And ready to go again
Because these folds are exquisite.
Only the phone equal
To the next spike
Blond euphoric
And so the names roll back
San Diego, Margate,
Margate, Kent.

Though nobody will vouch.
What we're talking here is compound interest
Which stands, at a certain vantage, for love in politics
You sit
You do nothing wrong
Maybe you go for a walk.
That way there's no redemption.

But it's not impossible
We assemble a line
Picture   a strictly ornamental universe
Geography   situationism
The twenty-four-hour news cycle
Your soul   at bay
You like it here
Don't you.

VII.

Lucked out   didn't we
That historic evening
When the angel of summer   waved the whole thing through
And you stood   outside the yard
Picking up the remains of the century
Assembling outbuildings
The way we asked them to be built.
Possibly.

                                        Remember nothing
                                        Immigration man.

I have this document in my pocket
Waiting to be rote
And I'm thinking if we could just do lunch
Maybe pick up something easy

                                        Recording equipment
                                        Is not allowed in the building.

Standing
Watching the trucks
Shake down the evening
Into particulars
                        Video evidence cannot be used in a court of law.
Please be aware
That any person
With picture taking capabilities
May not   this
Person
Dealt according.

The way the evening stepped forth –
This broken English
At the outbreak of the century
A sensibility at work
All singing all dancing
Only a notebook in which to annotate
Totally   unconvinced   by anybody's back-story.

VIII.

'Marcie' starts up.
Hello Marcie.
Marcie knows everything
There is to know about feedback.
She stands at the edge
Listening to the qualities
Of transmission
You stand alongside her
She pushes some kind of song.

On drums:
Max Ernst.
On bass:
Hannah Arendt.
Things to address directly:
The way the story ends.
Rubble.
Mediation.
Marcie buys a bag of peaches.
Eats one.
Hides the rest from the state.

You sing along with her
Some kind of dictionary of sensibility
In the right hands   it's a love thing
Hitting all the wrong notes
A siren, a cigarette
Sure signs of somebody's emergency
Riffing   when the song stops.
Marcie cuts her own hair.

Stands   outside the arcade
Learning to trust   the way a person tells it
As a blackbird locks down the skyline
Scarcely credible on such a scale
Only this is the way the story opens out
                    People clustered together in the Arab spring

Marcie   not confident of anything
Save some kind of reckoning
Occurring here.

Marcie

                                             A car horn

Did the percussion section leave you standing?

                                              A cigarette
                                                burning
                                      indecipherable
                                                  cause
                                        that extends.
                                         On rhythm:

Did you call a taxi yet Marcie?
Or did the footage persuade you
This is somewhere you could stay
At night
Lined up against the square
Though nobody said so
Capable   of a simple
Straightforward anger.

Marcie checks out.
The blackbird sings into
A person's whereabouts
In the city
Some person's washing
Leaving them hanging
In the wind to dry.
Air and such
While the networks go down
And you just standing
As the story breaks –
Still no letter
Only the operations.
Good to see you
Marcie

IX.

We should stay up all night
Watch the law   prosecute its business
Still no letter

                                        Walking the beach
                                Watching the aircraft drop
And you dance sometimes and I work
Because all this meantime
What else is there?

                                                To signify
                                Arms laid against him.
Still no letter. Possibly so.

                                Things to address directly:
                                        POLITICAL
                                        GEOGRAPHY
In the dooryard   momentarily   the traffic   stops
Too late for birds
And no sound happening
Of anybody's emergency
You smile   in another language
I sense a dance coming on.
Because there is space
Jarvis samples Arrested Development
Crowded only by the skyline
Not a measured room
And not stopped
                                Arrêté
We decline the implication
                                        One must not have a permit
Push the tables
Back.

                                He slept deeply until morning
                                Went out into the brilliant
                                        Threshold.
                        It's what we should pitch I think:
                        The ground is now the sky.

                                                        Jonquil.
                                                         Bones.
                                                  Breeze to zero.
                                        Streets   roof-tops.
                                          A person takes notes

Watch   as you dance
Foot out the architecture of the century
Co-ordinated in somebody else's neighbourhood
Only a history to call your own
Riffing   on the direction of travel
Silently annotating   the new geology
Pictures   told in three dimensions
                                Even by telephone in dead of night

Quietly   brilliantly
In all the available spaces
Dapper like the morning
In those telltale shoes
A rebuke confronted

                                with the structure of exception
Clockwise and   counter-clockwise
Turning.

X.

Still no letter.
I use the word *still* advisedly.
Still you say   *still*
Struggle to get the intonation right.
Stutter   over the doorway
A plane goes down
Airburst
People   gather before the wreck.

There must be something we can make of it.
You stand there radiant before the court
Explaining   everything
The moment you first came through
Impossible to frame
Only this *is* the way things happen

                                   Eyes set deep
                          Subjected to examination.

In this broken English
The sun sets laterally across the century
The fugitive lands
Crowd under separate names
Joined in semi-abstraction
You stand and regulate your bearing

                                        Airports
                      Certain outskirts of our cities

Hardly a way back through
Down along the Medway River
Strolling   annotating
Shipyards in the cold
Bystander taking notes
Down by the intersect
Where the language happens
Syntax
Forms like lilac
Where the uninvited

Stand in line.

And the radio fades
Nobody certain which way we're headed
You shrug
Maybe somebody somewhere
Assembled evidence enough
At variance with the theme
Some stack of mistranslations

                         Statements rendered unacceptable
                                     Inadmissible
                                           By the state.
But that's their story.

                                 Remember nothing.

I make a mappa mundi
To include this point.
Your story   air and such
                 stones   bearing
Doorjamb   at variance
Existing
Claim

SYNTAX

I.

I am holding my heart in my cheeks as the Americans say.
His absence is what the birds the waxwings sing about.
I can be straight about this
My method is to cut things out.
Days later I left a voicemail.
If you can
Call me.

As trees are my witness, the result was not anticipated.
They are right to observe the lyric is relational.
I count
Such shapes
Up in the streets the underground
No unpaid debts
This evening in the universe.

II.

I come back to it.
The lyric is the new geography.
I take this to be normal emotional
That all the co-ordinates are good.
Like that thrush
Picked up across the street
Aspects of a person's circumstance
Speaking plainly
It was a moment of intense legality.

What we're talking about of course
Is a genuine and subsisting relationship.
I count such shapes.
The truth of all such impasses
Is one has not found the form
And so I come back to it
The elementary mistake
Of translating 'we' as 'they'
Giving the impression
Always maintained
Shall comprise an area.

III.

You're looking good today I mean alive
To which we must address ourselves
As the earth turns
Trailing across the light of the sun
Which is one of the things I love
Fetching up a heap of bric-a-brac
A particular history
Deeply embedded
Plenty potentially

Which if we could co-ordinate it
Would come across
As a record of small civilities
Some of which may be inadmissible
No attempt made
Where it says excessively
Like moving from one pocket to another
In the street this morning
Continual change

IV.

You strike me as contemporary
I see you have all the attributes
Scuffed elbows and dirty toes
Subject to the say-so
As though we might
Fold back in
Picked up I mean
Registered etc.
To seek and

I mean thus
As though we might
Establish in accordance
Some kind of fictive theatre
Maybe would startle it into life.
In the street the plum tree
And on the plum tree
Waxwings
At work early
And now they
Range.

V.

With the utmost degree of intensity
The tree opposite
Across a wooden table
Accumulating books
La Medusa by Vanessa Place
Dance Writings by Edwin Denby
The ones I can see
At least and the term
Contemporary
Clear and
Unequivocal

It won't be.
That much we know.
It is a moment of
Maximum visibility
The bitter wind searching eagerly
Houses for which I can vouch
But can't quite see
The tree opposite
Backed by sunlight
Considerably disturbed
Something has left
The language.

VI.

That tree again
Which the birds left
And now come back to
May suspend temporarily
Companions of the earth
As one might say
This first day of spring
Now it is backed by sunlight
Itself
Against the crosswires
Like Cy Twombly.

Calm in the assurance
An everyday frame of life
Suspended maybe
In its entirety
A blatant opening up
Witness that tree
This day of all days
Disclosing itself
Against the wires
March 5th 2013
Approximately
Normal.

VII.

I find other materials
Feeling for the whole arrangement
From Dover to Calais
Not even
The traffic stops
And you told me about it
So now I know
I am a credible witness
As then as there
The underlying structure contributes

Other materials
To be carried out and
Used directly
Just such necessary measures
Like the workings of the feet
As the evidence checks out
Whoso extends
This evening
Listen
No invented house
No imaginary site.

VIII.

The simple thing to say is
The blackbird checks out
Set down on the white plane
Exactly where the public law stops
Something in the situation that would
Never have happened
I think to tell you that in change
Thought is made in the mouth.

The blackbird checks out
I assemble an elaborate voicemail
Made from work bricks and other materials
Employed to extend the sense of touch
Laths which
As such
May suspend temporarily
Like Twombly articulated by Agamben
Designated
Falling beauty

I go to designate the blackbird
He checks out without me noticing
I tell you
Using primarily
Strips of wood
Assemblages that extend
Bricks and other materials
Partial and incomplete
State movement
People

IX.

I walk away from the poem
It is an ok moment.
I'm like it's ok
And from the radio a quartet blares out
I guess
Though nobody says
I'm thinking it's an ok moment
Except for the echo
Which is strong
1827
Or thereabouts.

I work on the echo
I'm like ok ok
There are framing devices
That one day I'd like to tell you about
Witness context
A figure
In the transition between
And now I'm talking to the radio
This is not ok.

X.

I leave the following message
It is not ok
I speak with the implacability
Of the dead poet.
I call on Steve Collis of Vancouver
And my associates
The waxwings
Dear Jurisdiction –
Your conduct
Has become
Deplorable

I know it in my bones
It is past argument
I call on the trees and the
Street signs
As evidence
Echoing into place
A genuine and
Subsisting relationship
Here
Like houses
Shall comprise an area

XI.

May freely, safely
and without impediment
disturbance whatsoever
abide and trade
cross, stay
both by land and
any
and sea and
any
and may
and may

XII.

I write to you convinced
we shall comprise an area
it is a matter of holding
social space
open like a language
sometimes setting up camp
in the streets
the street signs
hammering
pots and pans

manufacturing an echo
something like
the evidence of intimacy
I write you through a language
remembering itself
partial and incomplete
across the noise which is
gathering
in the parks and
without impediment
keeping the powerful
awake

XIII.

I read into the night
Make notes on the new geography
Which is a series of interruptions
Partial and incomplete
And the waxwings that hold out
Making the analogy with collage
This evening in the lawscape
Only calm
Temporarily

Picked up in the street
The whole thing suspended in its entirety
Ensured in accordance
The everyday frame of life
This is my voicemail
I think we need other materials
Rectangular slabs
Bricks etc.

XIV.

Starting out
An observance
When a thyng is shapen
Something like
When the wind against
Sat down and made
A pull out map

On the common of No Man's Orchard
And many
Impartial

Duplicates
In the landscape

And then the wind
Drops

HERE

#1

The way it goes we should constitute the dooryard
Since we are here now by any reckoning

Adjacent to events that play out just
Off screen so I'm like Dartford maybe or Dover

Parts of Europe in the morning
I know people start from their beds.

I start from the dooryard. The principle is
The habit of some things happening,

Registering the way the planes go since
What we're thinking is a talkable space.

Not so much, just a sideline in exchange,
Sat on a couple of crates maybe the morning

After. Hash tag: frequency. Hash tag: left alone.
Stacking up the credits before the line goes dead.

Which is one of the ways. Think of it as
The exception not the rule. As rule, as

A way of working, listening to the traffic
As the drill starts up. So that whereabouts is

Barely the issue only the way we stand
In relation to bird song, close, the way

The trees outreach us still the way we'd
Like things having some effect. This.

A sort of setting out. I set out the dooryard
In front of you nobody proposing

The implications stop. Not an ocean, just
That here might do, blocking in the outskirts of

Some new economy. Has to. What else is there
Weather permitting a situation of sorts.

Which is a big ask. The dooryard is an
Unimposing space and one day maybe

We'll get the arrangement right.
I picture a republic of letters. Still there

Are birdsongs I can't name. I'd like to
Fabricate in language a place a person

Could stay. That's what I'd like.
A neighbourhood made out of

Roofs and windows. First Colin died.
I have no desire to make the traffic

Stop. There's this wren builds a nest
On the wall of the building stood

Opposite. And I tell you and we talk and
Somewhere the language holes up.

#2

So that everything is present.
Grass grows through cracks

In summer. There are paintings
By Bonnard in which a situation

Is an event, pressing things out.
I know places this isn't possible

My point being only the dooryard
Isn't one of them. More like an act

Of thought pulling all the details together
In some kind of document. I have visited

The archive and I will go there again but
The present is what we have stretched out

Like a case history in front of us and if you
Sit I guarantee you there'd be something

We could say. Start to pick up. Maybe just
A narrative of sorts. My point being only

The lilac is open now tuned to the event
Even as the letters circulate

Mis-pronounced and/or mis-directed
Barely even noticing the names. But

Binding even so see how the appleseed
Proliferates, pollen drifts in from the corn fields

Even as the goldfinches come and go. Even
As the planes go half loaded up watching as

The letter carrier hands round documents
Not stopping to talk catch up on the weather

Standing still and waiting as the lines join up.
It's the simplest request. I think that we should

Occupy the foreground, a sequence of voluntary,
Incremental acts, movements hosting space,

Lay out the furniture between us, bodies
Making an arrangement, getting all the gestures

Right. All the foliage pressed back. Call it
The choreography of presence. I imagine

A photograph taken after the event
In a non-descript yard, barely a chair

To sit on, ground wet like nobody
Noticed. After the transcript

Stopped. After the fact. Some setting
In which a context might be descried.

Here maybe. Hash tag: necessary.
Hash tag: talking it into place.

#3

The dooryard in question stands
Beside an ancient road. It is not

A polis although it is part of a polis.
Because of how it is positioned

It has no view except to say
Of roofs and windows framing

A restricted space. This is definitive.
It sets up discontinuities. A part

Of the polis that is its own preserve
As the road proceeds downhill

Passing towards the city gate
Which is not a limit though

We are not without limit.
This is the value of the dooryard.

It stands nowhere in particular.
It is a walled environment fronted

By an ancient road which if you
Walk down you pass the prison

Situated outside the city walls some
Kind of remainder dedicated recently

To foreign nationals. Making it a hub.
People come from miles around.

The road carries some of them
As it approaches from the coast

Like a series of concrete nouns
To which the syntax should be

Answerable. There is an emotion
Which is level and builds through

Semi-abstraction. We could itemise
The grounds. Here is the church.

Here is the steeple. Here are the
Barracks. Here is the glebe which

Maps show was once extensive.
Here is the curtilage marked by

Trees. This is where the verb
Phrases set things out subject

Frequently to reallocation. This is
The law. Here are the people.

Here is the lilac open in the yard. He
Spoke about it plainly to keep the whole

Thing sweet. Outwith. Whole thing
Notwithstanding. Sometimes on a good night

#4

Sometimes on a good night the language
Crosses over. Carries better. Crates.

A series of singular effects. We sat up till
Dark on a couple of crates somebody left

After piecing things together like sounds
Stories crossing over distributing syllables

As the ground went dark. Audible.
Open to a range of initiatives. Planes

Half loaded as the stars showed up
Against a background of wind and

Water open to a sequence of
Possibilities set down as indicators

In the polis in the dooryard we talked.
Late. The way things go. Set down

Evenly as context. The impulse is primitive
To report the names. Hyssop. Cigarettes.

One option is to accumulate images
Evidence surely of a meaningful exchange.

In private. I mean to say the impulse is
Basically lyrical. Words spoken privately

Thinking to be overheard. Which is politics
The way things go documenting structures

Of intimacy counteracting on a good night we
Crossed over into terms. Outwith. The way

Things go. The medium is roofs and
Windows. You sat there in the dooryard

Picking out the collared doves which
Dominate as questions asked and the

Answer is here now like anybody
Catching hold just figuring out the

Risks witness to the process as the
Light backs up. Like Margate light.

Witness the drift. This side of the
North Atlantic. Witness clapboard light

This side of Dover conscious of the
Framework we talked long enough.

Dogwood like some kind of subset
We sat on a couple of crates while

The ground went dark. Stars out.
Not admissible as evidence.

Nobody in addition. Till
The light held good.

THE ARCHAEOLOGY OF WALKING

It's what we should talk about, the poetics of space, and this room would be a place to start it, that we occupy and which people travelled towards over landscapes we can say we broadly recognize. Carrying a language built to name many of the key particulars – ook, firre, birch, aspe – as you might encounter them on the way maybe as the road drops into Harbledown and where the sky still comes big if you walk in early January and read it like a commons by which I mean carrying a language on the road into the city walking with a Canterbury bell through an entrance hall into the undercroft which would sometimes accommodate sixty, though they did build it for less than a quarter that many. There's the modern. Notice how the door swings shut. How it was necessary to approach with a different order of magnitude. Through Blean as the woods open out or maybe where the road meets No Man's Orchard knowing that an ende ther is so that in their wisdom the founders formulated an obligation. And I should say that when I say modern, I don't mean contemporary. And when I say occupy the language I mean figure the whole thing out. And when I say figure I mean it was on these rushes that the pilgrims slept, wall to wall, since the answer was given when the question was asked. At the door. Where all the evidence is of a language in transition. I come back to the geography of it: people in a landscape passing to and fro, by elm maybe or wylugh, people naming common objects. The politics of it: those signs you circulated are a living disgrace.

Ach. Those songs. Sometimes when I say poetics I mean politics. There's nothing complicated about it, watching the direction of travel, taking a decision to occupy the terms, since this is where the language takes shape and even as we use it we issue a new demand, outwith, registering the reality that we in are in fact the polis. Tasked with space. So that people would sleep in barns or under hedges and the principle was as they arrived there must be no exemptions, a way of journeying that became its own recourse, up from the Weald as it rises towards the view, the city looking back and nobody approaching could be unaffected. From the French, jornee. I like that image they have of the daily portion, which is really the measure is it not, that to which us alle is due. A day maybe like today and all the intervals marked in passing, carried with them, establishing a limit that is truly precarious. Naming things as they went, walking by chasteyn, lynde, laurer, maple, thon, bech, so that the geography of it framed the terms, not like any über narrative, but just like walking through it and picking things out, comprehending syntax as an effect of space. It's how they arrived. I mean, it's how they would arrive. I mean, somewhere in the early twenty-first century we obliterated the day. I don't blame Kenneth Goldsmith exactly but I want a language that gets how day follows journey, how movement through a landscape produces space. So that as they came down the hill after stopping in Harbledown, transformed by many and a history of talk, not one was refused and not one was unaffected and at the threshold they stopped and then they waved through.

Being a language in transition, for which we have to scour the landscape because those signs you circulated through the heat of summer bring us to a desolate pass, which is really the measure is it not, and the politics of it are truly precarious and we are on the brink and the badges prove it and the way the rhetoric sounds, all bets are off. So we cast out, since plainly the language isn't driven far enough, into said city walking collectively behind the orbit of the bell, which sounded as it goes and nobody who heard it could be unaffected and the charter laid out that they should write and read freely withal. Being a decision to occupy the terms. There is after all a grammar to a hostile environment. They would enter and at the moment of arrival the journey became a public event and what mattered was the way the day lay down, so that sometimes when I say politics I mean poetics, and sometimes when I say day I mean allocation and sometimes when I say journey I mean extent. That's the grammar. All the evidence is of a language in transition. They would arrive at the chantry passing through the woods at Blean carrying the day as they had watched it turn and sometimes they would name the increments, gathering the geography of it so that as they walked movement through the territory became a mandate. From terroir, the land, I mean being from the French, terroir, which is provisional and as they approached it how the city came into view, and the only way through is over the hill and I reckon the buildings must have looked magnificent, like a mandate, and as they assembled a sequence of actions became due.

The word is due. I say it like an archaeologist. I have no quote to offer only the observation that after they arrived they would sleep against stones, and that these were the terms in use so what they carried with them was a kind of entitlement measured by the day and the way they journeyed each one bearing an allocation of sorts. Which we can picture as a poetics of space constructed like a building we have forgotten to occupy. I say it like an archaeologist. People would walk here and after they had walked an entitlement became due, grounded in the grammar of the day so that how the limit fell was depicted otherwise, despite the discrepancy, people clockwise and counter-clockwise turning. Widdershins. Against the sun. With the sun and against the sun. Which the charter was bound to register since they were passing through and the principle was plain grounded as an act of language so that as they convened the messuage was opened and there might be no exemptions. Those were the terms. I mean these are the terms that they would occupy where the limit is as bodies rested on a stone floor after sweating towards the sun through the commons outside Harbledown and at the gate what they presented was a shared cause. Spoken like a bell. So that where we have the word messuage we might read the word dwelling house. So that as they stood at the threshold that had so wyde to turne the language would be thought to unfold because in passing this way what else is there? I mean at the limit. I mean in passynge people moving to and fro.

These are the terms. I say it like an archaeologist. To include, a requirement to make contact with a particular person in a particular way (including by telephoning a particular number) within a particular time period, being to limit, or otherwise make provision about Part 1, to enter. Includes premises used as a dwelling. Part 2, information: to be present at a particular time at a particular place. Part 3, oversight: to include land, building, and moveable structures where document includes a card or other means of recording. Where a person 'P' is liable to the following conditions and where information means a) about a person's external physical characteristics, including in particular fingerprints and features of the iris where it is visible and legible. Chapter 2, sham marriage. Chapter 3, miscellaneous, such as the taking of any interim or preparatory actions, unless the person demonstrates there has been a material change. Noting the form in which the evidence is to be supplied and noting the manner in which the evidence is to be supplied. To include the placing of a person on-board ship or aircraft. To include powers of entry. Insert 'pre-departure accommodation'. Insert 'Any other information about a person's physical characteristics.' Like hair colour. May specify only information obtained by external examination, being to include, as requested, outer coat, jacket and glove. In which it can be taken away. Insert 'and their parents etc.' Premises subject to these directions. For 'may' substitute 'must'.

The word is 'may'. What we have here is an archaeology of walking. They would start out in the morning and they would make their way across and all the permission they requested was the day which they would move their way into and as they walked they would occupy the landscape which as they named it the frame would pass. Speaking it like a bell. So what we have here are the common increments. So that as they made their way from Harbledown an entitlement became due which was carried with the terms and as they assembled laid out the language so that as they arrived and the buildings stood ready talking among them they started through. Which is like a syntax of sorts since largely it was a summer occupation started early as the allocation called for people walking together in the face of the sun constituting an arrangement it was necessary to maintain and as they made their way over the terms laid out so that this was common being a language in transition naming the particulars as the journey went. Specifying the terms. Ook firre, alder poplar birch apse, elm wylugh, chastyen lynde, holm laurer bech assh. One by one. To include the placing of a person. To include demonstration of material change. To include this as polis so what we occupy is syntax, to include land and buildings and moveable structure. Which is a threshold and as they arrived the bell would sound across it and as they showed up despite the discrepancy they would sleep against stones. To include powers of entry. To include physical characteristics. Being to limit or otherwise. Whan that song was songe.

FEEDBACK

#1

We are not done. After the April we had
And the August and the January, rain
Clean down against the dooryard steps,
Setting out the way the architecture
Separates things, places – persons,
Trees, bread – the way the documents
Stack up outwith the space set by
To read them, think how short time
Thou hast abyden here, airports
Certain outskirts of our cities, after
The process, the way the judgments
Foreclose; after the December and all
The elements left lying around us,
When the winds blow and the seas
Whose steadfast faith yet never moved,
Process, no change of rule only
The direction of governance, persons
Disregarded, after the borders
Closed; after the process, after
The wreckage in transmission, the rain,
The repetition, world without end,
In the streets we are not done,
This is unfinished business,
Outside standing, constructing space.

#2

This much we can say: insistence
Is part of the argument, coming back
To a person's bearing, the way a body
Rests, notwithstanding the story,
Was never man so like amonges us,
Separate, I don't believe it that
Chit chit chat. Part of the argument.
The dooryard echoes in winter
So the sound passes through
Of somebody else's emergency,
Abyden here, restricted in every
Particular. 'It was on the following
Day he fell from grace.' Within
A budding grove, a person designated
Uninvited. 'J'ai eu pitié des autres
Probablement assez.' I don't think so,
Hardly enough, so like my life
While it will last, the principle:
Elements shorn from context.
And somewhere we might stand
To contemplate an open
Environment; I learned something
Recently, that we lack tact
At our airports certain –
Part of the argument –
Talking simply, face to face.

#3

Then there is the question of
Measure, continuously monitoring
And modelling, in which circumstance
I want to specify blood and bone,
Gesture, motion, aught else the world
Can offer: a woman in the garden
Sings a cradle song. Trending.
A plane goes down. Maybe if we
Sift the fragments, lockdown on the
Skyline scarcely credible on such a scale,
Our all we have held together by spit
And syntax, moments in the process
When affection yields. Discourse.
I think we should sue today for no
Compassion, since these practices
Among us have functioned
Long enough, break open
The argument, the story that
Shuts up our territory: bodies
Governed outside the scope of law.
Subject to change. I get a call
About Dover, and in the garden
The lady singing gets our reports
To match. Sirens. Cigarettes.
She is a credible witness. Subject
To process. The sun kicks back.

#4

This is a song for lovers. The wreckage
Is part of the urgency. You send today.
Text me a scrap of life. Exact words.
Therefore simply does what is to be done.
Last thing: put some kind of document
Together. Something we can trade on,
The history of a conversation, broken only
By the moments the networks went down
As we talked, getting most things wrong,
Except perhaps the deep are done here.
Last thing: to exercise your faculties at large.
I live at the foot of a hill, look out over
An ancient city. At three in the morning
The traffic stops leaving only sirens
The way things go, echoing gracelessly
As we go. At four: birdsong. At six: start up.
And all the while process. Gesture.
Motion. Until his action is a reality
Long, long we sing by rote, shaping
To intervene. This is a song for lovers
And aught else the world can show.

#5

And the truth is there aren't many
Images. February. The news breaks:
The snow won't last. In the hoar frost
We contemplate obscure attachments.
Sleep pattern: broken. Future: indefinite.
And the realisation for like the millionth
Time, there is no context for the argument
To be put, which we should make only
A person presenting disparate attributes.
Notwithstanding a song thrush nails
The neighbourhood into place. And not
For the first time though this is snow
In February and where the letter
Finishes it doesn't say who wrote only
The way things go which is somebody's
Emergency: aggression rendered
In its most accurate form. With only
The process laid out. The laying out
Is part of the process. I lay this out:
I had to learn the simplest things last,
And I am writing to say that the buck stops
Where I stop. And the snow melts
And the context, falls into place.

Today is pale. I'd like to make
An intervention now please. Across
The city the traffic never stops
When the winds blow and the seas
And the small rain arbitrates the
Process and the waiting continues
And the watching, I'd like to interrupt.
From rupture: to break. I record that
A person's bearing is not now
Constitutional in a court of law
That the emergency is this,
The last book of songs and airs,
When we have wandered all our
Ways, the which on earth do spring;
Through cowslips and kingcups at certain
Outskirts of our cities, clustered
In bedless houses whereby the franchise
Stops, bordered, held at bay,
Not granted access to the currency.
Bid her therefore her selfe soone
Ready make. Bid her herself soon
Make, out of the fragments we left
Lying around us. Fragmentation
Is part of the process. Turning things out.
This is a song for lovers. Gathering,
Arbitrating, proposing tact.

#7

This is the object: to constitute
A modern document, put the pieces
Together in the open the way
The days fall out. You call after
You make your report. Reporting
Is part of the process. And the rain
Is. And the way the blackbird. You
Contemplate questions I decline
To ask. Even such is time. The object is:
To constitute a context. Where I live is:
The houses back towards an ancient
Church. Where Ethelbert married Bertha.
This is not my position. Questions not
Possible to formulate before a court of law.
Even such is time. Finding herself not
Twenty miles north of Dover where
The language stops and the jurisdiction
They called the building St Martins
Of Tours. A kind of welcome. A kind of
Gesture out. Even where the language:
Such is my position. Where the
Open, where the lilac falters,
Where a contemporary standing a
Contemporary stops. A welcome
Of sorts. We live in a pay-as-you-go
Environment and the contract is
Part of the process and I'm worried
One day the calls will stop. Such is time.
Even such is time. You call from
Outside the currency. And the rain is.
And the report. March 7th, twelve o'clock.

8

And so the reality is the process doesn't
Hesitate. In the garden a cat rips open
A garbage bag as the forsythia starts
To show which I can name now since
Somebody told me, in thick, blocky
Passages, the way a reckoning
Unfolds. And the way I reckon it
We should open with the untranslated
Born as I doubt to all our dole
With the morning in place since all
Was not unbeautiful suddenly holding
An emergency at bay. Suddenly.
Herewith. Outwith the politics
Notwithstanding. For none can
Call again the passèd time. You stop
You do nothing wrong I'd like to
Improvise a context, where with,
Somewhere where with lilac
Camped in conversation where
The dogwood lies. Here maybe.
Maybe herewith. Sometimes
The practice was outsourced to
Other territories. We look on.
We improvise the simplest things
Last. As the winds blow and the
Seas and the prospect starts again
Out of nothing as the dew starts as
The papers circulate making it up as
You go along.

#9

As you go as. As the seas. As you
Stepped over the threshold. As the
Winds as. As the traffic. As the
Emergency stops. As you wait as
Nothing happens. As you passed
Out of the currency. As the letter as
After the process after the aircraft
Drops. As the contract came good.
As a still more intimate model. As
Without restriction everything is
Lawful now. As the dew falleth
On the grass. As they pay you a deep
Attention, not even a compliment
As you go about your business
As for whomever inhabited it
As the story breaks. As the process
Sets out, as the framework
Sequences arbitrarily, as you came
From the holy land of a broken state,
Sirens, cigarettes, as the small rain
Graced the language, outwith,
Notwithstanding, as you spoke
We showed up late.

SOMETHING MY FRIEND

SOMETHING MY FRIEND

How it goes is
Something has left the language
Something leaving has left the language
And so the language is resolved
Something has left and in leaving
Has left the language
Unaltered
Something leaving has left the language
And therefore the language is composed

As in the outline of an event
And as it is tolde
Impartial
Which if it could write
Might record a promise
When the time is
Comes all at once

Something left
Witness the language
Think of it like
Duplicates in a landscape
Like lyric
Constituting syntax
Forming a politics
One by one

through ▪ **prep. and adv. 1.** Moving in one side and out of the other side of (an opening, channel, or location). ➤ so as to make a hole or opening in (a physical object). ➤ moving around or from one side to the other with (a crowd or group). ➤ expressing the position or location of something beyond (an opening or an obstacle). ➤ so as to be perceived from the other side of (an intervening obstacle). ➤ expressing the position or location of something beyond or at the far end of (an opening or an obstacle). ➤ expressing the extent of turning from one orientation to another. **2.** continuing in time towards completion of (a process or period). ➤ so as to complete (a particular stage or trial) successfully. ➤ from beginning to end of. **3.** so as to inspect all or part of (a collection, inventory, or publication). **4.** North American, up to and including (a particular point in an ordered sequence): *they will be in London from March 24 through May 7*. **5.** by means of (a process or intermediate stage). ➤ by means of (an intermediary or agent): seeking justice through the proper channels. **6.** So as to be connected by telephone. ▪ **adj. 1.** (with reference to public transport) continuing or valid to the final destination. ➤ (of traffic) passing from one side of a place to another in the course of a longer journey. ➤ (of a road) open at both ends, allowing free passage from one end to the other. **2.** (of a room) running the whole length of a building. **3.** (of a team or competitor) having successfully passed to the next stage of a competition. **4.** *informal* having no prospect of any future relationship, dealings, or success.

Origin: Old English *thruh* (preposition and adverb), of Germanic origin; related to Dutch *door* and German *durch*. The spelling change to *thr-* appears circa 1300, becoming standard from Caxton onwards.

Pronunciation: θru

ACKNOWLEDGEMENTS

A number of the poems assembled in this collection have appeared or been performed in other settings. An earlier version of 'Through' was written for a collaboration with Simon Smith and Jack Hues & The Quartet, featuring Jack Hues, Sam Bailey, Mark Holub and Liran Donin. The poem was published in *Cordite Poetry Review* and a recording of the collaboration appeared in *Thinking Verse*. 'Feedback' was written for a collaboration with Simon Smith, Sam Bailey, Evan Parker and Matt Wright. The collaboration was performed at the Sounds New Poetry festival in 2012 and was published in *Blackbox Manifold*. 'The Archaeology of Walking' was written for a collaboration with Nancy Gaffield entitled 'The East-bridge Variation' and was performed at the Eastbridge Hospital, Canterbury as part of Sounds New Poetry 2014. 'Syntax' was first published in *The Evergreen: A New Season in the North: Volume I*. It has been a privilege to work with all the writers and musicians mentioned here and it is a pleasure to have the opportunity to thank them. I am very grateful also to the editors who have been generous enough to publish my work.